TOGETHER
AND LIKING IT

by Lynn Lott, M.A., M.F.C.C.

and Dru West, M.A.

THE PRACTICAL PRESS
PETALUMA, CALIFORNIA 9495

Published by:

The Practical Press
P.O. Box 2615
Petaluma, California 94952

ISBN 1-882033-06-4

Printed in the U.S.A.

Cover Design by Hal Penny

Dedicated to

Hal and Joe

TABLE OF CONTENTS

INTRODUCTION

We find rest in those we love, and we provide a resting place in ourselves for those who love us.

St. Bernard of Clairvaux

Marriage is a beginning, not an end. It can provide the opportunity for men and women to talk to each other without the roles and images that keep them from knowing each other as people. If we really listen to what men and women want from their marriage, we find they both want the same thing: to be loved and accepted.

Marriage is a process, not a solution. It's an opportunity to be totally and genuinely involved with another human being. In a healthy marriage no one can be a spectator. Both partners must be participants. No one can sit on the sidelines while the other partner works at being married.

Many people view marriage as a relationship where two incomplete people become one whole person. This kind of thinking has led many couples to form relationships that stop individual and couple growth, which leads to marital and individual dysfunction, pain and disharmony.

In this book, marriage is viewed as the decision of two people, each a complete individual, to add positive strength to a common lifestyle. The goal of this relationship is to nurture and cherish the other-- as each would cherish himself or herself--and to provide a safe harbor which honors growth and change.

The basis of a healthy marriage is mutual respect and love. The activities we've presented here can help build both of these qualities or clearly point out areas where they may be lacking. As you work together, you'll be getting information from your partner or giving information about yourself. This information is not for arguing about, for correcting or defending. The idea of giving and getting information is for you to share your individuality with each other. Listen to each other. It doesn't mean you agree or that you see things the same way. You don't have to agree, but you do need to listen and learn as much as you can about yourself and your spouse.

If you find you can't listen without getting hurt, defensive or argumentative, then this workbook may not be the place for you. If you're feeling that defensive, or if it's that important for you to make your partner change his or her mind, you may need to be in therapy, not a self-help group. There may be other issues that are going to get in your way of learning right now.

The material in this book focuses on your relationship, not on being a parent. You may find, however, that if you can work out issues as a couple that a lot of the problems you have about kids, in-laws, whatever, will work out from there. If you want to learn about parenting issues, we suggest that you do find a group to help you study the ideas and skills you want to develop as parents.

HOW TO USE THIS BOOK

This book has three purposes:

1. to teach concepts and skills to encourage couple closeness,
2. to serve as a workbook,
3. to use as a training manual for leaders of couple classes.

The activities here will help you become aware of your thoughts and values about yourself, your partner and your marriage. The material is divided into six sections, which can be used by you and your partner at home or in a two-hour class for couples. The seventh chapter gives information about how to lead classes. If this book is being used for a couple's class, we suggest that all group members read this chapter so that everyone understands the structure and format needed for group work.

MAKING CHANGES

The activities in this book are designed to help you and your partner work together to improve your relationship. Although one person in a relationship can work to make changes, the purpose of the material in this book is to increase communication and understanding for BOTH partners. Working and talking together will speed up the change process.

Keep in mind that reading this book is a clear indication that you are committed to making changes. As committed as you may be, that process is difficult. You may unconsciously continue to do a lot of things not to change. Instead of fighting with yourself to make change, focus on what you can learn. Instead of being angry with yourself, say to yourself "This is how I think." "These are my values." "Isn't it interesting that this is how I see things." Or, "Isn't it interesting that this is how my partner sees things."

If you do want to make changes, realize that change is a process. The first step is to become aware. The changes you want to make will take time. No one changes overnight. Remember, it's not "Can I change?" but "Will I change?" Throughout this book we'll be showing you, again and again, that the only person you can change is yourself. When you change yourself, you will be inviting your partner to respond differently, but his or her choice to be different is up to him or her.

Before you begin this book, you might want to make a deal with yourself that your goal is to learn as much as you can. Use the things that help you and forget the things that don't. Let yourself be a learner.

IF YOU'RE NOT MARRIED

This book was written for couples who want to learn and practice the skills for mutual respect and equality in a relationship. Although the word married is used, we believe that these activities will help any two people in a relationship. When you see the word married, just substitute the word relationship.

Good luck and enjoy!

CHAPTER I

UNIQUENESS: WHO AM I? WHO ARE YOU?

AND WHAT MAKES US SPECIAL

AS A COUPLE?

Every marriage is made up of two individuals who come into a relationship with their own ideas, attitudes, beliefs, backgrounds, hopes, expectations, wishes and histories. Many of us married with the mistaken belief that most of our partner's thoughts and ideas were the same as our own, and that if our partner truly loved us, then the thoughts and ideas that weren't like ours would change over time--or that we'd be able to change them to be like our own.

All of us have different thoughts and feelings, even when we have similar backgrounds. Your ideas, expectations and thoughts are unlike any other human being's. Your partner's ideas, expectations and thoughts are as unlike yours as yours are unlike anyone else's. You may like the taste of strawberry ice cream; your partner may not. You may like the color green; your partner may like a color you hate. You don't taste or see the world in the same way.

 Although you experience the world in different ways, you may still agree but for different reasons. You may want to paint your house green because that color brings back wonderful childhood memories of your grandparents' house. Your spouse may want to paint the house green because no one on your street will have a house that color. Your similarities can be based on differences.

Differences and similarities make your relationship unique. No other couple in the entire world will be able to duplicate the relationship you create with each other. The more you can understand your partner's way of tasting, smelling, hearing and seeing the world, the better your relationship will become.

In this chapter, as in all the others, we'll be asking you to share your thoughts and feelings with your partner. As you watch and listen, get in touch with the fact that things that happen near you are not necessarily about you. The things your partner says, thinks, and feels are statements about her or him. Notice if you take what your spouse says or does personally. If you do, you may get into a defensive mood. Instead, develop an attitude of curiosity about your partner--and yourself.

INTRODUCTORY ACTIVITY

HOW I SEE YOU

This activity will help you and your partner learn how you both see each other. Although it's meant to do in a group, it's worth taking the time to do this together at home. You'll need magazines, glue, paper (white or colored) and marking pens.

Create a collage name tag, cutting out those things that remind you of your partner. Glue these on and write your partner's name somewhere on the paper. Give this collage to your partner.

When your partner gets the collage, he or she is to write, on the back, the first five things that came to mind when he or she saw it.

PROCESS: What did it feel like to create the collage? How did you feel when you gave it to your partner? How did it feel to get it?

LEARNING ACTIVITIES

ACTIVITY 1: **THE TOP CARD**

From *To Know Me Is To Love Me*. Reprinted with permission from Lynn Lott and Marilyn Kientz.

As long as things go our way and we don't feel threatened, we do just fine. We coast or meet life's tasks. But when we feel threatened, we've all learned a way to respond that we think will protect us, save our ego, and get us off the hook.

We do this response on "automatic pilot," without giving it a thought. The response is called our Top Card.

The following activity will help you find your Top Card. Once you're aware of what it is, you can notice when you play it and what happens when you do.

Circle the ribbon of the box that has the things inside that you would most want to avoid.

Stress and Pain	Rejection and Hassles

Criticism and Ridicule	Meaninglessness and Unimportance

If You Choose:	Your Top Card is:	And Perhaps You:
Stress and Pain	Comfort Avoidance	Make jokes, intellectualize, do only the things, you already do well, avoid new experiences
Rejection and Hassles	Pleasing	Act friendly, say "yes" when you mean "no," give in, worry what others want more than your own needs
Criticism and Ridicule	Control	Hold back, boss others, organize, argue, get quiet and wait for others to coax you

Meaningless and Unimportance	Superiority	Put down people and things, knock yourself, talk about the absurdity of life

The irony of the Top Card is that we play it to avoid something, and the thing we're trying to avoid happens anyway.

PROCESS: Ask your spouse to give you as many examples as possible of ways you play your Top Card. Remember, your Top Card is not who you are but what you do first when you're feeling scared or stressed.

Examples:

For Top Card of Control: Your partner might say, "I notice that whenever we talk about something painful that you want to change the subject. Or, "I notice it's hard for you to talk about your feelings."

For Top Card of Pleasing: Your partner might say, "I notice that you ask me permission to do things rather than telling me you're going to do things" or "You take care of me instead of yourself."

For Top Card of Superiority: Your partner might say, "I notice that sometimes you say things that are putdowns to me" or "I notice you get easily overwhelmed and try to do too much at once."

For Top Card of Comfort: Your partner might say, "I notice that you don't finish your sentences" or "I notice that it's sometimes hard for you to try new things."

ACTIVITY 2: **SELF- ASSESSMENT QUESTIONNAIRE**

Clarifying how you think and feel at a specific time can often help you work towards the future. On a separate piece of paper, write out your answers to the following:

A. Why am I reading this book?
B. What are my hopes for us?
C. What positive feelings do I have about you?
D. What positive feelings do I have about us?

E. I like myself when. . . . (Fill in as many items as you
can think of.)
F. I don't like myself when. . . . (Fill in as many items
as you can think of.)
G. How do I feel about myself right now?
H. What are my feelings now about being more open
with you?
I. Name three times when I've felt closest to you.
Describe those feelings.
J. Which feelings do I find most difficult to share with
you?
K. How do I feel when we make love?

PROCESS: Share your answers to this questionnaire with your
partner.

ACTIVITY 3: **LETTER TO SELF**

Another way to find out about your expectations is to write a
letter to yourself about what you'd like to get from this book.
Include a change you'd like to see in yourself and a change you'd
like to see in your relationship.
With your opposite hand--the one you don't normally use--
write how you defeat yourself from getting what you want.

PROCESS: Share your letter with your partner.

ACTIVITY 4: **SPECIAL CONTRIBUTIONS**

A healthy self-respect for what you bring to your relationship
is vital for any marriage. Every person brings special talents,
skills, attributes and interests to his or her marriage. On a
separate piece of paper, list the special contributions you bring to
your relationship. To help you identify those contributions, you
might think about what would be lacking in your relationship if
you weren't there.

PROCESS: Share your list with your partner.

ACTIVITY 5: **BAGGAGE**

When you married, you brought different backgrounds,
attitudes and experiences into your relationship. One way to get
in touch with your differences as individuals is to write out the
messages you got as children about the following and to compare

them. Many of the attitudes you acquired as children are the attitudes you carry with you today.

On a separate piece of paper, write the messages that first come to mind when you think of the following subjects:

Children
Money
Work outside the home
Where to live
Vacations
Sex
Love
In-laws
Friends
Household chores
Add your own!

PROCESS: Share your responses to each of the items with your partner.

ACTIVITY 6: **FAMILY CONSTELLATION**

The family that we grew up in is the place where we formed patterns of relating to others, especially our peers, which we still carry with us today. Many of us are unaware of how much we still behave in ways we saw ourselves as children or behave differently from the way we saw our brothers and sisters. Our personality was most influenced by our siblings. We tend to marry someone like the sibling with whom we competed, not someone who is like our mother or father. Only children can remember someone who was a chief competitor--a parent, cousin, or child in the neighborhood.

To find out how you saw yourself and others, draw a picture of the family you grew up in with each person saying something. Give the picture a title, and list 3 or 4 adjectives to describe each person in the picture. On the back of your drawing, list 5 to 10 adjectives to describe yourself now and 5 to 10 adjectives to describe your spouse.

PROCESS: Share this picture with your partner or in your group. Exchange pictures and see if you can see any similarities in your families of origin and your couple relationship. Don't analyze, but do give comments and feedback about what you see. (I noticed, I felt, I wondered.)

ACTIVITY 7: **HOW WE MET**

It would be very surprising if you and your partner told the same story of how you met. It is absolutely normal to think of and remember the meeting differently. It doesn't mean that your spouse forgot how you really met or wasn't there if his/her memory is different from your own.

Write the story of how you met your partner. Allow yourself room to have some fun with this. If you're sitting with your partner, don't look while your partner writes his or her story. When you're finished, give your story to your partner and have him or her read it out loud. As you listen to your partner's tale of how you met, notice how different your perceptions are. If you have a hard time with this, it may help to think of yourself as being in a play. Remember, Romeo stood in the garden, while Juliet stood on the balcony. Their perceptions about what went on were different because their points of view were different. All the players don't see the same scene from the same position. You may wonder if you were in the same play. That's normal. It's okay. It's just interesting.

PROCESS: How different were your perceptions? Why would they be different? What types of things did your partner remember that were different from your own?

ACTIVITY 8: **LIKING YOUR MARRIAGE MORE**

Creating an honest relationship with your partner requires that you acknowledge the things you wish were different about your marriage. Stating what you wish would happen or what you'd like to see in your marriage does not mean either of you have to do the things you talk about.

To help you open up to each other, write out what it would take for you to like your marriage more. Begin your sentence with "I'd like my marriage more if . . . ." Take a minute to pretend you already have it. How are things different?

Now, imagine that you have three wishes and can change any three things in your marriage. What would you change?

PROCESS: Share your answers. Set a timer to limit discussion to five minutes each. If you're in a group, allow an additional five minutes for group sharing.

ACTIVITY 9: **MAPS OF YOUR MARRIAGE**

A map of your marriage will help you get a quick picture of where you are currently. In the circles below, fill in the percent of time you and your spouse spend on the following partner tasks:

Work
Kids
Couple fun
Family vacations and fun
Exercise/health
Logistics of household management
Friends outside the family
Extended family
Time for self

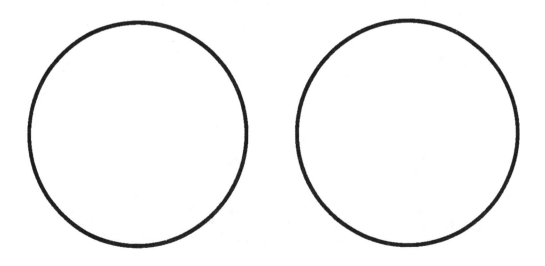

HUSBAND   **WIFE**

PROCESS: Notice areas of imbalance. Is there too much or too little time, or an area too weighted for one partner? Discuss these with your partner. What are you learning about who you are as an individual and as a couple?

SUGGESTIONS FOR GROUP SHARING

Discuss any of the activities. Share your experiences, questions or feelings.

NOTES:

CHAPTER II

UNDERSTANDING:

LEARNING HOW EACH OF US THINKS ABOUT THINGS

Love does not dominate; it cultivates.
Goethe

In the first chapter you began to look at your own uniqueness as individuals and as a couple. You're cultivating an attitude of curiosity. In this chapter you'll be developing more ways to encourage your partner to share and listen without either of you feeling that listening means agreeing.

You've begun by putting yourself in your partner's shoes and seeing that your partner experiences the world differently. You're more aware that what goes on inside your partner is information about him or her. You need this information to understand your partner's thinking. Otherwise, you'll be living in a blind. That is, you'll be assuming that your partner thinks and feels as you do when he or she really doesn't.

Acknowledging your differences is the most important step. It'll help you with all the chapters to come.

The key to a successful marriage is mutual respect. That is, for each partner to say honestly to the other, "You have the right to your ideas, attitudes, opinions and actions. I may not like everything about them or agree with everything about them, but you have the right to them. And I have the right to my thoughts, actions, opinions, and feelings."

When there is respect for each other, there is room for differences. Differences aren't bad. Once they're accepted you may decide to work towards solutions to problems based on those differences, instead of giving in, compromising or giving up.

Two people who respect each other know in their hearts that both partners are good enough just the way they are. Without mutual respect as the foundation it is very difficult to have a long lasting relationship. Love for each other or communication skills is not enough.

INTRODUCTORY ACTIVITY

THE LOVE PROTOTYPE

Every person forms a marriage with his or her own ideas about love. As a child, you learned to feel loved in certain ways. Your partner also learned ways to give and receive love. Ironically, your partner may be showing you a lot of love in ways you miss, because they don't fit your picture of what love is supposed to look like.

To help you clarify how you each give and feel loved, think back to when you were a child. How did you show your parents that you loved them? Put those things under the area called SHOWS LOVE BY. Now, what did your parents do to make you feel loved? Put those things in the area called FEELS LOVED WHEN.

For example, Marc's parents showed him that they loved him by reading stories and working on models with him. Marc showed his parents he loved them by bringing home good grades and awards for school accomplishments. June, Marc's wife, remembers her parents showed her that they loved her by baking cookies for her and bringing home little treats. She showed her parents she loved them by giving them hugs and kisses.

Marc feels loved when others do things with him. He shows love by achieving. June feels loved when she gets little treats. She shows love by being affectionate.

WIFE

Shows Love By: Feels Loved When:

13

HUSBAND

Feels Loved When: Shows Love By:

PROCESS: Share what you learned with your partner. Has your partner been doing things that you missed as signs of love? Make a copy of this chart. Post it where you can see it every day. When your partner does one of the things he or she learned as a child to show love, recognize that's the highest compliment your spouse can give you.

If you aren't able to think of ways you showed or received love as a child, you may not know that you ARE lovable. In that case, you might want to work with a counselor to help you learn ways to feel loved and to develop patterns for showing love.

LEARNING ACTIVITIES

ACTIVITY 1: **LIFESTYLE**

Each of us carries around memories from our childhood which can give us information about how we see ourselves, others, and the world. These early perceptions are the basis for unconscious basic beliefs. Although they were formed in childhood, we often live our adult lives as though they were truths. They become rules--or portholes--through which we view life. Understanding our early beliefs can help us become aware of unconscious attitudes.

For example, Sue remembers back to when she was four years old. Her grandparents came to visit. Her mother spent the afternoon cooking a ham dinner, while her grandmother taught her silly songs. The men--her father and grandfather--went out to the garage to look at something.

This memory gives Sue information about some of her unconscious beliefs.

I have fun with someone else.
Others know how to do things.
Women cook and sing. Women teach me.
Men are interested in things outside the house. Men
do things together.
Life is exciting.
Therefore, I can have fun and learn from women who do
the cooking and singing, but men do things together
outside the house.
A news headline of that memory might read:

Sue finds life exciting by cooking and singing without
men.

What you can learn about yourself? Think back to when you
were a child. Focus on one memory. Write it out, word for
word. Now, see what information your memory gives you about
the following:

> I. . .
> Others. . .
> Life. . .
> Men. . .
> Women. . .
> Therefore. . .

PROCESS: Share your statements with your partner or another
couple in your group. Give and get feedback from each other.
Given that you hold these beliefs, how would they help or hurt a
relationship? With the help of your partner or the other couple,
come up with a headline or summary of your beliefs--something
you can easily remember--to help you see how you come across to
the world.

ACTIVITY 2: **INVITATIONS**

This activity will help you develop your "attitude of curiosity"
for those times when your partner makes a judgment or a
statement about you. If you're like most other people, you
probably shut the door to communication and understanding by
becoming defensive rather than being open and inviting. For
example, one partner may say something like "You're so sloppy
about where you put your things away." A typical response of
someone hearing a statement like this is to feel hurt and to want
to defend or attack in return. A response might sound like
"Well, if YOU wouldn't keep changing where things go, I

wouldn't have such a problem putting things away. Besides, you're so fussy."

As you might imagine, a conversation like this is going to escalate into hurt feelings on both sides. Some people attack, some defend and others simply close up. But the result is the same. Communication and understanding have stopped.

When you have an attitude of curiosity, you want your partner to give you examples--more information. Being curious, you want to gather information about how others see you. You WANT to learn more about yourself. You remember that listening does not mean that you agree. And you understand that validating your partner's feelings does not mean you have to change, fix the problem or problem-solve. It's easier to stay curious if you remember that what is said about you is NOT who you are. It's just information about how you may be coming across, and it's information which will help you understand your partner better.

First, to help you become aware of your own behavior and to help you get in touch with how you stop communication, ask your partner to make a statement or judgement about you. Have some fun with this. Instead of actively listening, try defending, attacking or closing up.

PROCESS: What did you learn about yourselves? Which style of stopping communication felt the most natural for you?

Now, to get in touch with being curious, ask your partner to make a statement or judgement about you. You can use something he or she has said before or something new. In this step your partner needs to risk sharing honestly with you. For example, your husband says, "You're such a spendthrift." Instead of arguing or fighting, ask for more information. Say, "I didn't know you felt that way. Tell me more about it." Then listen. Ask for specific examples, and listen some more. Say, "What are some ways you think I do this?" Listen. Ask, "Is there anything else you'd like to add?" Then listen again. Finally ask, "How does this make you feel?"

The purpose of listening is to gather information, to help clarify what your partner's issue really is, and to learn about yourself. In the above example, the issue may not really be that you're a spendthrift. It may be that your partner wishes he could spend more money on himself, but doesn't feel comfortable doing so. However, because you always end in a fight, your partner may never get to learn about himself--or herself.

Follow these ground rules to keep communication open:

1. The purpose of listening is to learn, not to fix.

2. Only one partner is to make a statement or judgement at a time. Save the other partner's turn for another time. If you take turns, it will feel like your partner is paying you back for what you said.

3. It's extremely important to let each other know how much you appreciate your openness with each other, to thank each other, and to share how much you love each other.

4. If the partner who is listening starts to feel a lot of pain, STOP. Don't continue at this time. It's perfectly all right to stop and to try again later. Do try to notice what defenses came up.

Now, here are some suggestions of what you can say:

Really? I didn't know you felt that way. Tell me more about it.

Could you be more specific?

What are some ways you think I do this?

Is there anything else you'd like to add?

How does that make you feel?

Thank you for sharing with me.

PROCESS: What did you learn about yourself or your partner? Were you able to stay curious, not angry or defensive?

ACTIVITY 3: **FILLING YOUR LOVE CUP**

This activity will help you remember that mind reading does not work. Many of us think that asking for something means that it isn't as good. If our partners really love us, they'll know what we want. If they love us, we wouldn't have to ask. Contrary to popular opinion, when you ask for something, it's just as good as having somebody guess what you want.

Why ask for what you want? Because if you give, and give, and give, you'll empty out your energy and your resources. You need to have things put back into your cup. However, when you ask for what you want you've got to be clear. If you ask for what you want, you might even get it. You're going to learn how nice it is not to wait for your partner to mind read.

Write down as many ways as you can to fill up your cup. For example, your list might include having time for yourself, getting a massage, going shopping, getting help with the dishes, getting a hug, having your spouse notice how hard you've been working and acknowledging it.

Share this list with your partner. Ask your partner to do one of the things from your list within the next week or day.

PROCESS: How did it feel to make the list? To share it with your partner? How did it feel to ask? What might you do if your partner says no?

ACTIVITY 4: **CREATING A SAFE HARBOR**

This activity will help you open up to those areas where you are vulnerable and help you clarify what you really want from your partner when you're feeling down or discouraged.

Write out on a piece of paper the following sentences, filling in the blanks:

What I would like from my partner when I'm feeling down and discouraged is. . .
(A specific behavior, such as a hug, or saying, "I know you'll work it out.")

When my partner is feeling down and discouraged, I assume that he/she wants. . .
(A specific behavior, such as distance, for me to talk to him/her about it, etc.)

What my partner does that really hurts me is. . .
(A specific behavior, such as leaves the room, rolls his eyes.)

The dirtiest weapon I've got for jabbing my partner is. . .
(A specific behavior, such as acting like he's the problem, or judging her behavior.)

PROCESS: Share your answers with your spouse.

SUGGESTIONS FOR GROUP SHARING

Discuss any of the activities. Share your experiences, questions or feelings.

NOTES:

AND MORE NOTES:

CHAPTER III

DEPENDENCE, INDEPENDENCE, INTERDEPENDENCE:

THE COURAGE TO LET GO

Many men and women marry with the belief that two half people become whole when they marry. The idea behind this belief is that you're not a complete person--you're not good enough-- unless you find a partner. Through your partner, somehow, you're supposed to get all the things you don't have and experience all the things you've never experienced. This kind of attitude turns your partner into a crutch that you have to keep nearby at all times. You can't go too far away from each other. You have to cling to each other so you can operate in the world. This kind of relationship is dependent. It's suffocating, smothering, debilitating, and dysfunctional. It stops growth. Without growth you don't have health. Dependent relationships hurt everyone.

What do we mean by dependency? At the base of dependency is fear. At worst, it's fear that says, "If I let you go, you'll leave me, and if you leave me, I'll die." It's not accepting the fact that you are alone. And that you are a capable, complete individual. Once you can accept your aloneness--and your wholeness--you can be with others in ways that nurture them and yourselves.

Dependency is an excuse for not looking at your own behavior. It leads to blaming others, making others responsible for your options, and looking for excuses, instead of doing the things you need to do in your own life to learn and grow. Life is a process with many lessons to learn. No one can learn those for you.

Most couples want a relationship that is interdependent: where decisions are based on agreements, not assumptions. Agreement can only be reached when each partner has the opportunity to share his or her feelings and thoughts. Assumptions are, at best, a guess. When you are interdependent you recognize that you and your partner may have differences, and that these enrich the relationship and help the partnership. There is cooperation, trust, respect, and joint decision-making.

You can't go from a dependent relationship to an interdependent relationship without first becoming independent. If you're in a relationship where the two of you are very dependent, you'll need to start growing yourself up: having courage and faith in yourself and your spouse, taking risks, trying new things, and letting go of your partner.

INTRODUCTORY ACTIVITY

DEPENDENCY

If you're not in a group, this activity will be a little harder to do, but it must be physically acted out to achieve full emotional understanding. Don't just read about it, do it!

One partner be an "A," another a "B."

1. B's hang on necks of A's from behind. B tries to walk. (See how much I need him.)
2. A leans back like ironing board; B holds A up from behind. (See how strong I am; no one can tell I'm secretly supported.)
3. A and B face each other, one walking on the other's toes. (No one can ever come between us; we'll always be together. Look how free we are.)
4. A and B back to back, arms linked. (We've got all angles covered; we're not dependent because we look out to the world.)
5. A and B put one leg together, hip to toe, arms around each other to become three legged. (We're dependent, but it doesn't show much.)
6. A and B put palms together. A walks backwards, keeping balance with B. (See how rebellious I am and how dependent you are.) (Point out that what you oppose owns you.)

Did you notice that in all the activities that if one acts on his/her own that the relationship crumbles?

NOW, stand at a distance you are comfortable, facing your partner. (An interdependent marriage requires space and the other's presence.)

Where do you fit in your present relationship?
What do you have to do to get to where you want to be?

PROCESS: Discuss how you felt in each of the sequences.

LEARNING ACTIVITIES

ACTIVITY 1: **APPRECIATIONS**

One way of encouraging independence and interdependence is to take time to appreciate each other. However, if you're dependent, you might feel insecure about your own worth.

If you don't think you're good enough, then you are probably putting yourself down, criticizing yourself and believing that you're nothing. You need to appreciate and encourage yourself! The better you feel about yourself, the more you'll be able to appreciate your partner's wonderful qualities and the more you'll be able to give appreciations to your spouse.

Think of an area where you are being negative with yourself. Write it down. Now, with your partner's help, turn that negative self-talk into a positive statement. For example, if you tell yourself "I'm disorganized," your partner needs to turn that statement into something positive. (For example, "You're a capable person. It's okay to do one thing at a time" or "You can let yourself take small steps.") If you say, "I never make enough money," your partner could turn that into a positive statement. (For example, "Your worth is not determined by how much money you make" or "We'll work it out.")

Say your new positive statement to yourself three times a day.

PROCESS: Turning negative statements into positive ones is often difficult. Share what you learned with your partner.

ACTIVITY 2: **COMPLIMENTS**

Others may compliment you, but often you don't get to hear the things you really want to hear. For example, you may want to have your spouse tell you're a great entertainer. Your partner may be telling you that you're a great cook, or that you're a great interior designer, but that's not what you'd really like to hear.

To help you identify the compliments you'd like to hear, write three things you'd like to have recognized about yourself. Give this list to your partner and have him/her say, "I appreciate (your item). For example, I really appreciate what a great entertainer you are."

Say, "Thank you" to your partner. Give him/her a hug and say, "I love you and I'm glad I married you."

PROCESS: Share your experience and feelings with your partner or with the group.

ACTIVITY 3: **DEPENDENCY CHECKLIST**

This activity will help you assess how dependent you are. Rate yourself on a scale of 0 to 5. (0 means yes, 3 means sometimes, 5 means no.)

A. Do you refrain from giving orders or taking orders from your spouse?
B. Do you allow for separateness from your spouse?
C. Do you believe that the happiness of your partner is up to him or her?
D. Do you say what's on your mind even when it may upset your partner?
E. Do you say no to your partner when you want to?
F. Are you able to try new things without asking for permission from your spouse?

If your partner left you tomorrow, could you deal with the following:

G. The kids?
H. The inside of the house?
I. The outside of the house?
J. A job?
K. Your own laundry?
L. Your car?
M. The checkbook?

Add up your scores and plot yourselves on the graph below:

Independent   **Dependent**
(0)   (65)

25

ACTIVITY 4: **MARRIAGE AS CHOICE**

The decision to stay married is always a choice, just as it is when two people decide to get married. Ask yourself the following question: "If my partner never changes one bit from how he/she is today, would I still want to be married?"

If your answer is no, then your decision to stay in your marriage IS a choice. You can stop trying to make your partner change, because you can't change anyone but yourself. You can do the things you need to do to enrich your life, or you can leave your partner and create a new relationship with someone else.

If your answer is yes, but you still don't like some of your partner's behaviors, recognize that you're also staying in your marriage BY choice. You can, however, change yourself to enrich your own life. You need to recognize that you cannot make someone else change. Your partner's change has to come from his or her own desire to change.

PROCESS: Discuss your answer with your partner.

ACTIVITY 5: **CONTROLLING YOUR PARTNER**

This activity will help you understand the impossibility of trying to control your partner. You can do the activity with corn meal or by visualizing the process.

Take a box of corn meal and pour some onto the palm of your hand. Your assignment is to contain and control it. If you squeeze your hand real tight, what will happen? If you leave your hand real flat, what will happen? What happens when you cup your hand just a little bit? What are ways to leave room for your partner and to let him/her know where your outer limits are?

PROCESS: Discuss with with your partner or in the group how this activity relates to marriage.

ACTIVITY 6: **PLACATING**

In a relationship there is a need for honest feedback about each partner's limits. Each partner really needs to be clear about those limits with the other. If boundaries aren't defined, then resentment will develop. And resentment leads to revenge, hurting each other and anger.

Take a few minutes to close your eyes and imagine that you have a large balloon filled with air. The balloon is your boundary, and someone is pushing into it. Every time that person pushes, he or she is demanding something from you or is pushing you too far. You don't say anything, and the person keeps pushing. What will happen if this happens over and over? What if you never let the person know where your boundaries are by saying, "Stop, I can't handle this" or "I don't like that"? (Pretty soon the balloon bursts. That's the end of the balloon.)

PROCESS: What are ways you placate? What are the ways you don't tell your partner where your boundaries are? Create a statement for yourself to use with your partner, such as "This is my boundary, and I'd like you to know it" or "I can't make you do such and such, but this is how it is for me." Practice saying your statement to your partner.

ACTIVITY 7: **ASSESSMENT OF DEPENDENCE/ INTERDEPENDENCE**

This activity will help you see where you fit in your relationship based on how dependent or interdependent you see yourself with your partner. On a separate piece of paper, complete the following two statements with as many items as you can think of:

A. If it weren't for (Your spouse's name), I. . .
B. Without (Your spouse's name), I couldn't. . .

PROCESS: Share your lists with your partner and with another couple. Ask your partner or with another couple to help you decide whether your statements are dependent or independent.

A dependent statement will have clear sex role definition, express fear, excuses, blame and guilt. It will include ways in which an individual stops himself or herself from growing. An interdependent statement will show the relationship as a safe harbor, providing help to each other, cooperation, mutual respect, courage, risk taking and honesty. For example, "If it weren't for George, I could develop my career" is a dependent, blaming statement. So is "If it weren't for Marsha, I could go fishing." On the other hand, a statement such as "If it weren't for George's encouragement, I wouldn't have tried out for that management position" shows risk taking and courage, as does "If it weren't for Marsha's encouragement, I might not have gone on that great fishing trip in Alaska."

SUGGESTIONS FOR GROUP SHARING

Discuss any of the activities. Share your experiences, questions or feelings.

NOTES:

CHAPTER IV

COMMUNICATIONS:

BEING ASSERTIVE AND RESPECTFUL

The opposite of love is loneliness.

In the previous three chapters we've been asking you to share your thoughts, beliefs, ideas and feelings with each other. In this chapter we'll be looking more closely at communication. Communication, however, has been greatly overrated. It was once thought to be the only cure-all for every unhappy marriage. And that if you learned another way to put words together, or if you learned the right gimmicks, that you'd then be communicating.

Real communication occurs on a deep level. Unless you have mutual respect, you won't be able to communicate. You won't be able to do the deep listening required to hear the intent of what is being said. Intent comes from a place other than our mouths.

Most of the communication we have is from our heads in the form of judgments, rationalizations, and analyses. In a couple relationship, partners need to communicate from their hearts and guts with honesty. This honesty has to do with the courage of taking a risk by revealing yourself. When you're respected, you feel safe to say anything. When you respect the other person, you want to hear real feelings out and to understand where they are coming from.

Although you have feelings, you don't have the right to say things that are hurtful. Honesty doesn't mean being abusive or hurtful. You can be angry and love someone at the same time.

Communication can be a wonderful, powerful tool to help you tear down the barriers between you. Not talking about things is very lonely.

INTRODUCTORY ACTIVITY

SPEAKING FROM YOUR HEART AND YOUR GUT

When you are able to speak from your heart and gut, you'll feel an intense relief which is very different from the sensations felt when you speak from your head. Speaking from your head refers to rationalizations, judgements and observations, instead of speaking from the deeper levels of your heart and gut. Because of the opportunity for feedback and discussion, this activity is intended to be done in a group. But you might want to try doing it at home. If you find that it's too hard to understand or do at home, then save it for a time when you are in a group with other couples or in therapy.

Think of something you would really like your spouse to hear, something that you have gone round and round about, but that you believe your partner has been unable to hear. Pick one of those things that you feel so frustrated about that you almost feel like giving up.

With the group to give you feedback as to whether you are talking from your head, your heart, or your gut, tell your partner what you would like him or her to hear.

First, briefly--in one or two sentences--speak from your head. Tell your partner what you want him or her to hear. (Group members are to give you feedback as to whether you are in your head. That is, making rationalizations, judgements, observations, etc.) For example, I wish you'd make a budget so you'd know what your expenses are.

Now, place your hands over your heart. Say the same thing to your partner, speaking from your heart. (Group members are to give you feedback as to whether you are still in your head. If so, try again until you are.) For example, It's hard for me when you don't bring home more money. I feel pressured and worried about paying the bills.

Now, place your hands over your stomach. Say the same thing to your partner, speaking from your gut. (Group members are to give you feedback as to whether you are speaking from your head or heart instead of your gut. If you're not speaking from your gut, try again.) For example, I'm angry that you pay others before you pay yourself. When you're broke, it puts extra pressure on me to find more money.

PROCESS: Discuss the experience of talking from your head, heart or gut. Could you feel the differences in your body?

LEARNING ACTIVITIES

ACTIVITY 1: **ARE YOU SAYING?**

Partners often say things to one another before we clearly understand the issues ourselves. This activity will help you and your partner clarify and understand what your partner is trying to say to you. Your goal is to ask questions that start with "Are you saying. . . ?" until your partner give you three "yes" responses.

For example, suppose your spouse says to you, "I really miss having you here when I get home from work." Your task is to ask as many questions as necessary about that statement until your partner answers yes three times. You might ask, "Are you saying you don't like me working?" (She answers "no".) "Are you saying you feel lonely without me? (She answers "yes".) "Are you saying you'd like me to quit my job?" (She answers "no".) Are you saying that you find it hard to walk into an empty house?" (She answers "yes".) "Are you saying you'd like to come home later than I do?" (She answers "yes".)

When you have three yes answers, stop. You now have more information about what your partner really meant by the original statement, so does your spouse.

PROCESS: Share with your partner how this activity differed from your regular style of listening.

ACTIVITY 2: **MARRIAGE CONFERENCE**

Every couple needs to take time to discuss issues and problems. But often the communication breaks down because each partner doesn't have a chance to speak freely without interruptions.

Set a time to be alone. Each of you is to have ten minutes of UNINTERRUPTED listening. Keep your mouth shut while your partner is talking. Whatever you or your partner says during this conference time is not to be talked about until the next conference. If you're in crisis, do this activity once a day; otherwise, you can plan for a weekly meeting. Each partner has full use of all ten minutes, even if he or she has nothing to say.

(It's often surprising that after a five minute silence something comes up.) Make sure there are NO distractions.

ACTIVITY 3: **JUST SAY "NO"**

Do this activity with your spouse, each taking turns. Ask your partner for something. Your partner is to say "no," without explanations, excuses, or whatever. You are to try to manipulate your partner into saying "yes" by whatever means you can think of.

PROCESS: After you've both had a chance to practice being manipulative, discuss the ways that got to you the most. If you were the one doing the manipulating, what were some of the things you used? Did you use them as a kid? What was it like to say "no"? Was that hard for you? Think of some areas in your life where what you learned could help you.

ACTIVITY 4: **NOTES**

Communicating with notes is another tool which can help your relationship. Create a note you would put under your partner's pillow or in his/her lunch. Think of a note you'd write if your partner promised to do something and forgot. What would it say?

ACTIVITY 5: **STARTING AND STOPPING WITH THE SAME THING**

This activity will help you become more aware of what you do to avoid dealing with the real issues in your relationship, and how you might be keeping yourself in arguments that go round and round by sidetracking. That is, instead of working through the issue, you might change the subject, generalize, catastrophize, attack your partner, get angry, or put the issue off until a later time. The following example shows how sidetracking works:

Wife: "I don't like to always call the babysitter."
Husband: "I'm reading the paper and would rather talk later."
Wife: "I understand that, but the last 18 times I brought this subject up you've found a reason not to talk. I need to work this out."
Husband: "Ever since you started going to that class, you've started making demands."

Wife:	"This isn't about the class. This is about babysitters."
Husband:	"Well, I think it's ridiculous that they cost so much."
Wife:	"I appreciate your concern, but I would like to create a list of babysitters and take turns calling them when we need one."
Husband:	"I'm tired of all these charts, lists and schedules."
Wife:	"We still haven't worked this out. You're sidetracking the conversation and we need to work this out."

In this activity, one of you is to tell the other something that you want to talk about. The other is to try every possible way to sidetrack the issue. The partner who wants to talk about the issue has the job of not letting the other sidetrack. Bring your spouse back to the issue until it's talked about.

PROCESS: Discuss what it felt like to sidetrack your partner. What did it feel like to have to keep bringing your partner back to the issue?

ACTIVITY 6: TEN WORDS OR LESS

Communicating can be wonderful, but talking too much is a problem for many couples. Instead of going on and on about an issue, tell your partner in ten words or less what you want to say. For example, "I'm angry that there wasn't any gas in the car," instead of "John, I've been meaning to talk to you about the car. I went out to use it today, and when I climbed in and started the engine, guess what I found?"

As you talk have your partner count your words and stop you at ten. Keep trying until you can complete your message in less than ten words.

PROCESS: Discuss this activity with your partner or with the group.

ACTIVITY 7: WATCH MY LIPS

It is especially useful when you feel your partner isn't paying attention to what you're saying to point to your lips and say,

"Watch my lips." Keep repeating it until you have his/her full attention.

Practice a few times. Got it?

PROCESS: Could you use this technique?

ACTIVITY 8: **SELF-TALK**

Hearing yourself unload all the talk in your head about an issue is one of the most supportive things one person can do for another. However, many of us believe that when others ask us to listen that we have to give advice, observations, and comments. Usually, what they really need is a good ear.

Ask your partner to give you a few minutes of his/her time to be a sounding board, without offering help, suggestions or feedback. Talk out an issue that is bothering you. As you unload all the things that are going on in your head, you'll often be able to hear things that give you a better understanding of yourself and the issue. If you're the one listening, do everything you can to keep your mouth shut--even if that means placing your hand over your lips.

Take turns practicing. One talks, the other listens-- without any feedback, observations or comments.

PROCESS: Was it easier to talk or to listen? What did it feel like?

ACTIVITY 9: **ARGUING EYE TO EYE**

Arguing is one way couples stay distant from each other, but disagreements don't have to create walls between you. Decide to have an argument about anything you want. Give each other eye to eye contact-- hold hands or touch as you do.

PROCESS: Share what it felt like to have physical contact during an argument. Did it feel harder to argue? What about looking at each other eye to eye?

ACTIVITY 10: **STEP IN YOUR MATE'S SHOES**

Many of us believe we understand our partner's point of view because we imagine ourselves in their shoes. To really understand our partner, we need to see from his/her position, understanding how it feels to be him or her.

In this activity, one of you is to talk about something that is bothering you. The other is to reflect back what is said. For example, if one partner feels hurt that he/she wasn't invited on a boating trip, the listener feeds back the statements in the following manner:

> You're feeling . . . (hurt)?
> You're wishing . . . (I'd go boating with you)?
> You're thinking . . . (I don't care about you)?
> Did I get it right?
> If not, what's the part I missed?
> Do I have it?
> Do I understand it?
> Have I missed anything?

Show your partner that you are in his or her shoes!

PROCESS: Share what it felt like to be heard or to listen?

ACTIVITY 11: **INTERRUPTING**

Interrupting and talking for your spouse is one sure way to break up communication. So, with your partner, talk about an issue while the other interrupts and talks for the other. Take turns being the talker and the interrupter.

PROCESS: How did it feel to be the one being interrupted or having your spouse talk for you? What did it feel like to be the interrupter? Does this happen in your marriage? If your partner is interrupting you, could you find a nonverbal signal to give your spouse so you can continue your conversation?

ACTIVITY 12: **INCOMPLETE SENTENCES**

Some of us have difficulty saying what we really feel, especially when we come to the painful or difficult part. A person who is having difficulty doesn't need help finishing his sentence. He does need encouragement and help to express himself with his own mouth, and with his own words.

In a marriage, painful feelings need to be talked about. If you can learn to help your partner say what he/she feels, you'll be moving towards deep understanding.

With your partner, each taking turns being a talker and a listener, role play a person who can't say the painful or difficult part of the sentence. For example, talker says, "When you went out the other night, I was . . . " (The real feeling or painful part is blocked.)

The listener is to go back to the beginning of the sentence and say, "When I went out the other night you were. . . ? What comes after the you were?" The listener DOES NOT fill in the blanks. If the talker says, "I don't know" or "I can't remember," the listener asks, "Could you try to remember?"

Keep repeating until the talker can say the painful part.

PROCESS: How did it feel to be the talker or the listener? How did it help you to have your partner go back and repeat your sentence if you were the one who couldn't finish the thought? Does this ever happen in your marriage? Could you use this to help each other?

ACTIVITY 13: **UNSOLICITED OPINIONS**

There are going to be times when your spouse really doesn't want to know what you think or feel. In a respectful relationship the partner giving unsolicited opinions or advice will find it far more productive to ask "Do you want to hear what I think about that?" If your spouse says "no," don't say things he or she doesn't want to hear. Appreciate your partner's honesty.

Taking turns with your spouse, spend a few minutes to practice asking "Do you want to know what I think about that?" The other partner practices saying "no."

PROCESS: How did it feel to say "no"? Was it hard or easy? What about being told "no"? Do you give advice or opinions to your spouse when he or she doesn't want it? Could you use this activity in your marriage?

TIPS FOR MARRIAGE COMMUNICATION

ESTABLISH A WEEKLY COUPLE MEETING TIME: Many couples don't take time to talk about issues that really bother them. They figure they can squeeze time into a few minutes each day, but usually the issues don't get worked through. Then they become so huge that they cause arguments. Instead, make a date, once a week, to meet with your spouse to talk about issues and feelings. During the week write down issues you'd like to discuss--this will become your agenda. Set a weekly time and a time limit. Use this time to gripe, talk, plan, share, work on issues, and appreciate each other.

MAKE A DATE TO TALK: Some issues may not wait for your weekly couple meeting time. If you have something you want to talk about, be respectful of your spouse's ability to listen. Ask, "When would be a good time for us to talk?" Or, "Is this a good time to talk?" Your spouse may have other things on his/her mind at the moment or have things to do. That doesn't mean he/she doesn't love you or want to listen.

FIGHT IN A PUBLIC PLACE: For some couples, feelings may get so intense during discussion of an issue that one or the other says or does things that are disrespectful, or that stop communication. Discussing an issue in a public place provides the needed incentive to remain calm and respectful. Make a date with your spouse to work through an issue at a restaurant, the library, a museum, or some other place where you would become conspicuous if either of you acted disrespectful towards the other.

SUGGESTIONS FOR GROUP SHARING

Discuss any of the activities. Share your experiences, questions or feelings.

38

NOTES:

CHAPTER V

CONFLICT:

DIFFERENCES AND PROBLEMS

There are probably as many techniques for conflict resolution as there are diet books. However, if you don't have conflict resolution tools based on mutual respect, then you don't have true conflict resolution. You know there's mutual respect when you have agreement to resolve the conflict. Agreement speaks with actions, not with words. Anyone can say, "Yes, I want to work this out with you" with words, but it is actions that really speak. This is why you need to listen to what a person does, not what he/she says. If your partner says, "I want to work this out with you," but argues, puts you down or backbites every time you say how you feel, or if you say you want to work it out, but you're not willing to hear his/her point of view, then you really don't have agreement for conflict resolution. You have agreement to keep the conflict going.

When you use the conflict resolution tools you learn in this chapter, notice that when you argue, defend, attack, or blame that you are in agreement to have conflict, not conflict resolution. If you find yourself in one of these conflict activities, you'll need to say exactly what you see. For example: "We"re fighting," or "We're arguing." "You're getting defensive," or "I'm feeling like rationalizing right now." "All I want to do is blame you." Make an observation about what's going on. Deal with that, and try to get back to agreement for resolution. There's no use continuing any technique unless you can agree to resolve the problem, not aggravate it.

One way to work towards agreement is to adopt the concept of a "no-fault marriage." Instead of looking for who's to blame or who's at fault, focus on the problem. Improve the situation. Assume that both of you are right instead of trying to find someone at fault.

You may have experienced past hurts that you've never shared with your partner, or you may have shared them, but are continuing to hold on to them. These can only hurt your relationship and the intimacy you want to achieve. You might want to ask yourself "Is this old, hurtful memory helping me have a better relationship now?" Chances are that it's only helping you stay angry, hurt and distant from your partner. The skills you're practicing here will help you and your partner find ways to talk about unresolved conflicts. No one can change the past. What you do with past hurts is up to you. You can, however, learn constructive, positive ways to be with each other now and in the future.

It's not useful to try to resolve conflicts by ignoring them, avoiding them, or pretending that fighting is not part of a loving relationship. There are ways to fight fair and there are ways to fight dirty. Conflict is part of living together and resolving conflicts is a very important part of intimacy. You cannot have intimacy if you avoid dealing with conflict.

Sometimes you'll realize that you made a mistake. If so, say you're sorry. It's not a sign of weakness to acknowledge that you're human.

INTRODUCTORY ACTIVITY

CONFLICT RESOLUTION

To begin understanding conflict resolution, let's look at your conflict skills. With your partner, start trying to resolve a conflict. However, instead of worrying about using the proper steps, each of you is to act as defensive, blaming and argumentative as you can. Get in touch with the feelings and look at the results.

PROCESS: What are those feelings like? Could you recall them later to help you remember how it feels to work towards keeping up the fight, instead of resolving it?

LEARNING ACTIVITIES

ACTIVITY 1: FEELING WORDS

The first step in letting your partner know how you feel is

to be as clear as possible about your own feelings. The best way to be clear is to be as brief as possible. The following sentences can help you frame your feelings. They are:

> I feel . . . .
> I feel . . . because . . . .
> I feel . . . because . . . and I wish . . . .

For example, let's suppose that you and your spouse are planning to landscape your new yard. You sit down together and start writing down ideas to give to the landscaper, but every time you mention something you want, your spouse chances the subject. You feel really upset, because you feel ignored. You can let your partner know how you feel by saying, "I feel ignored." You can be even clearer by expanding on what you're feeling by being more specific. You can say, "I feel ignored because you changed the subject when I suggested planting a tree in the middle of the deck." Now your partner has a better picture of what's going on for you. You can expand on that by saying, "I feel ignored, because you changed the subject when I suggested planting a tree in the middle of the deck, and I wish you'd pay attention to my ideas too."

Try it. One of you be the talker and the other the listener. The talker fills in the blanks of the following sentences. If you can't think of a feeling, use the feelings chart at the back of this book.

1. I feel . . . .
2. I feel . . . because . . . .
3. I feel . . . because . . . and I wish . . . .

Now, the listener needs to feedback what the talker said. So, practice the following sentences with your partner, filling in the blanks with what your partner said:

1. You feel . . . .
2. You feel . . . because . . . .
3. You feel . . . because . . . and you wish . . . .

PROCESS: How much clearer was this than your old style? Did you feel heard? Did you understand what your partner said?

ACTIVITY 2: **EARLY MEMORIES**

Recollections of early memories often help you learn about your personal issues. You may find yourself remembering some childhood event, especially when you're angry. The issues that are the basis for anger usually have to do with one or more of the following:

Recognition
Power
Justice
Skills
Equality
Responsibility
Self-worth

Although you may not see the connection at first, early memories can help you become aware of the "baggage" you bring from your childhood.

For example, you've just gone out to dinner with another couple and the other couple paid for dinner. You notice you're feeling angry with your spouse because she eagerly relented when the other couple insisted on paying the tab. You remember that when you were a child you went out to dinner with your parents and their friends. Your father insisted on paying for everyone's meal after a great fuss and playful tug of war over the check. You remember how everyone laughed when your father finally pulled the money out of his wallet and handed it to the waiter. You remember your own sense of security and pride about your father's insistence.

This memory would be giving you information about what you believed about yourself, others or the world. These early beliefs might include the idea that the man in your family pays for and takes care of others or that others don't pay for your meal. It might also be that you believe there's supposed to be a friendly argument about checks or that it's up to the men to insist.

What does your memory tell you about beliefs you might still be carrying with you? Think of a recent time you were angry. Now, close your eyes and get an early memory. Remember, it may not seem to connect. Write down your memory. What is the memory trying to tell you?

PROCESS: Share your memory with your spouse. Think about what you believed about yourself, others or the world based on your memory. Ask your partner to tell you what he/she might believe if that were his/her memory. Now, look at the list of issues that are usually the basis for anger. Which of these were you angry about?

ACTIVITY 3: HELPING EACH OTHER

There may be times when you don't understand your own anger. Your spouse can be a resource to help you clarify your thinking. In this activity, think of a time you felt angry. Tell your spouse, "I'm angry and I need your help because my anger is getting in my way. I'm not sure what my issues are. Would you listen to me and feedback what you hear? Give me your ideas about why I might be angry?"

Talk about your anger while your spouse listens. When you're through, listen to his or her ideas. Let your partner help you look at what else might be going on for you. Your partner's job is to clarify, not argue. If you want to reverse the process, let some time pass or it might feel like revenge.

PROCESS: Share what you learned about yourself and your partner. How did it feel to be the listener? How did it feel to get feedback about your anger?

ACTIVITY 4: MONEY ISSUES

Money is one area where couples have problems at one time or another. Write down an issue you have about money. (For example, she forgets to write checks in the checkbook or he has a bigger allowance than I do.)

If you're at home, pretend the issue really belongs to your neighbor, not to your partner. Ask questions of your pretend neighbor about why he/she thinks or feels the way he/she does about that issue. Remember that if you start fighting, then you're not pretending!

If you're in a group, collect the cards with issues from all members and put them into a pile. Each member draws a card out of the pile, making sure that it's not his/her own. Take turns reading the issue and having the group members share things they've learned to deal with that issue.

ACTIVITY 5: CONFLICT RESOLUTION STEPS

Talking out issues with your partner isn't always easy. You may find that you're more interested in saying what you think or believe than in listening to your partner. A simple outline for structuring your talks can help.

1. State an observation, such as "I noticed that you fall asleep at my parents' house. I wonder if we could find a way to deal with this?"

2. Ask your spouse for his/her point of view. Say, "What do you think?" or "How do you feel about it?"

3. Feedback what your spouse said. For example, "You feel bored going there every Saturday night."

4. State your feelings and view of the problem. For example, "I feel guilty if I don't visit them because I'm their only child, and I'm concerned because they're alone."

5. Ask for suggestions. Say, "Can you think of something we can do so we both feel okay?" Brainstorm ideas!

6. Pick a solution you can both live with for a short time-- one day, one week. For example, "I'll drop in on them in the afternoon, and we'll go out to dinner by ourselves afterwards."

7. Agree on a date to see how it worked. Say, "Thanks."

Think of an issue you'd like to work out with your spouse. Follow the steps outlined above.

PROCESS: Share what you learned about this process with your partner or in the group. How is it different from your normal conflict style?

TIPS FOR WHAT TO SAY WHEN NEGOTIATIONS BREAKDOWN

1. There will be times when you want to share your feelings, but not want help with the problem. Many of us think we have to fix someone else's feelings. It often helps to say, "I'm angry, and I'd like to tell you so you'll know, not so you'll fix it."

2. Instead of guessing what your spouse thinks and feels, try asking, "What's your picture about . . . ?" Be responsible for letting your partner know how you feel or think by asking, "Want to hear my picture?"

3. Remember, in a "no-fault" marriage, if there is a conflict, you're both right. Say, "We have a conflict. Let's work it out so we come up with something we BOTH can live with."

4. If you find yourself continuing to fight instead of resolving the conflict, stop. Let your partner know how you feel. You might say, "We're not getting anywhere and I feel sad. I want to be close and this conflict is in our way." Another way of stopping the fight is to say, "You just want to fight. How will that help?"

5. Giving in is not respectful to you, your spouse or your relationship. If you see either of you giving in just to stop the fight, say, "It's not okay for either of us to give in. We both need to feel okay."

6. If an issue repeats itself, then you might need outside help with the problem. In that case say, "We fight about this all the time. We need help working it through."

7. Two people do not have to agree. As a couple, you do need to find ways to respect each other's views. There may be times when you need to say, "I'm entitled to my feelings and so are you. We don't have to agree. How can we go on from here?"

SUGGESTIONS FOR GROUP SHARING

Discuss any of the activities. Share your experiences, questions or feelings.

NOTES:

CHAPTER VI

TIME TOGETHER:

FROM FOOLING AROUND TO QUICKIES

FOR BEING A COUPLE FIRST

If you think back to your courtship, the first thing that most of you will remember is how much time you spent with each other. Before your lives got complicated, you made time to be together. In fact, you probably thought you couldn't live without each other for five minutes. You called each other on the phone. You broke dates with other people to be together; you didn't want to be with anyone else--just each other.

When you were together, you did romantic things. You walked down the beach, or took long drives in the country, held hands and bought each other little gifts. Then you got married. You got busy and had children. You got busier. You had fights. And pretty soon you started taking your relationship for granted.

Taking a relationship for granted is the first step towards the end of it. A relationship needs nurturing. Your kids, your plants, your dog, your goldfish, everything alive--including relationships--need care and attention.

Up until now in this book you've been working on learning who you are and who your partner is. But what about your relationship? For it to survive, you need to spend time together. There are a lot of different ways to be together. Let's look at some of them.

INTRODUCTORY ACTIVITY

SOMETHING I LIKE TO DO

The amount of time you spend with your partner is not as important as the quality of the time. Many couples spend a lot of time together fighting or being lonely in the same house. You can be together and do your thing in a sharing way.

To help you focus on what you really like to do, make a list of five things for each category below:

Things I like to do alone.

Things I like to do with friends.

Things I like to do with my mate.

Once you've made your list, code it. When was the last time you did that activity. (Within the last day (D), week (W), month (M), 6 months (6M), or 1 year (Y)).

Pick one area to improve. Brainstorm with your mate. Make a specific plan with your mate--with a date and time--to do one of the things on your lists.

PROCESS: What did you learn about yourself? About your mate?

LEARNING ACTIVITIES

ACTIVITY 1: **TYPICAL DAY**

Write out what you do on a typical day. Star those things you do with your mate, and put a star by the things you wish you were doing together.

ACTIVITY 2: **WHAT WE CAN DO**

Many couples say they can't go out because of the cost. They forget that going out together can cost a lot or it can cost nothing. With your partner, brainstorm a list of things you can do together using the following divisions:

Free

Under $5

Under $10

Under $20

Under $50

Under $500,000 (What the heck, let's spend our kids' inheritance.)

PROCESS: Set a date with your spouse to do one of the things on your list.

ACTIVITY 3: **WAYS IN WHICH WE SPEND TIME TOGETHER**

Take a few minutes to list ways you spend time with your partner. Next to each item, write out the things that stop you from wanting to be together? Now, if you're in a group, take turns role playing the following situations. If you're at home, talk with your partner about what you would feel in these situations.

1. A discouraging welcome home.

2. Parallel play/work that has quantity, but no quality. (Both at home together, but no emotional connection.)

3. Children who interfere with couple time.

4. Using time together to punish or lecture.

PROCESS: Share your list with your partner.

ACTIVITY 4: **SEX GAMES: FUN AND UNFUN ONES**

If we're really honest with ourselves, we can admit that sometimes we do and say things that don't encourage couple closeness in bed. The purpose of this activity is to increase awareness of patterns of behavior which invite distance instead of intimacy. As you look over the list below, see if any of these have ever happened in your marriage. If so, think of specific times they've happened and talk about it with your partner.

	PARTNER A:	PARTNER B:
1.	Kisses, tickles, hugs or rubs B's back.	Assumes that this is the first step toward having sex, whether he/she wants it or not.

Result: B avoids contact with A; A feels rejected and hurt.

2.	Makes the same moves every time, ending in his/her own orgasms, without any consideration for partner's needs or without any inventiveness.	Lies there passively angry, wishing it were different, but going along with the same program every time.

Result: Build up of hostility, martyrdom and unresolved anger in partner B.

3.	Says, "Let's make love."	Says, "I'm not in the mood, because we had a fight" or "The children might hear" or "I'm busy right now" or "Because" "Because" "Because"

Result: No sex until the one day of the year when everything is right for partner B, whether partner A needs it or not.

4.	Brings home a can of whipped cream	Says, "Have you been reading those filthy magazines again? I don't do THAT kind of thing!"

Result: Whipped cream goes sour and so does the marriage.

PROCESS: Were you able to see yourself in any of the above scenes? Can you add any other examples to this list? Share your answers with your partner or with your group.

If you would like to change any of these patterns, go to the next activity.

ACTIVITY 5: **ANOTHER WAY OF LOOKING AT THINGS**

Most of us have at some time or another thought to ourselves "If only my partner did X, then it would be better and we'd be closer." Another way of understanding closeness is to look at our own feelings, what we do, how we think, and what happens as a result. An improvement in closeness usually results because of a change in our own attitude or behavior, not because of changes in our partner.

Changing a feeling is difficult to do. But if you can change a behavior or a thought, the change in feeling will follow.

For example, Sally had been working hard all day at the office. When she got home all she wanted to do after dinner was to relax and read. Her husband was really interested in being close. In fact, he had been thinking about going to bed early that night. When he approached Sally, she felt irritable, told him "Leave me alone. I'm tired." Tense and abrupt, she behaved in a way to distance herself from her husband.

Sally's thoughts probably sounded like this: "If I say "no" I'll be a bad wife for not wanting to please him. He wants to have sex, but I want to be alone. If only he'd understand me." The result of these thoughts and her behavior made Sally distance herself from her husband, instead of moving closer.

Changing Sally's behavior or attitude DOES NOT MEAN she's to agree to have sex when she doesn't really want to. But she could change her attitude or behavior about being approached for sex when she's tired and wants to read. Her attitude and behavior can invite closeness without sex. Sally could tell herself, "I'm not a bad partner for not wanting sex or for needing some "alone" time." She could give her husband a hug or kiss, sit with him for a few minutes to cuddle, tell him about her reasons for not wanting to have sex and her need to read. She would then be meeting the needs of the situation with her husband AND her own needs.

To help you think about ways you can change your own behavior or attitude, think of a recent time when you didn't want to be close. Write down what you were feeling, thinking and doing.

What attitude or belief could have changed?

What could you have done or said to let your partner know what you were thinking or feeling in a more loving way?

What could you have done to meet your own needs?

PROCESS: Share your answers with your partner.

ACTIVITY 6: **TALKING ABOUT SEX**

Many couples have no problem at all talking about chores, what to have for dinner or what to do on the weekend. But when it comes to sex, many couples hold back from sharing desires and wishes because they're afraid of hurting their partner's feelings or ego. Certainly, talking about sex CAN be a lot more threatening than talking about what you're going to fix for dinner. But holding back in sharing these feelings and wishes STOPS couple closeness and intimacy from growing.

Listed below are some topic areas you can use for discussions to help you learn more about yourself and your partner. They're listed in order of least threatening to most threatening. Decide on an area to talk about that is comfortable for both of you. Set a time to talk when you won't be interrupted. It's wiser to talk about sex outside the bedroom--and away from the bed.

LEAST THREATENING

Talk about the messages you got about sex when you were a child.

Talk about things you're curious about or were curious about as a child.

Talk about the sexual beliefs, feelings or experiences you had as a child.

Talk about what you like or don't like sexually now.

MOST THREATENING

PROCESS: Give each other ten minutes of uninterrupted time to share your answers. Also, share your feelings about talking about any of these areas.

HINTS AND ACTIVITIES TO IMPROVE TIME TOGETHER

1. **PILLOW TALK**: Use the time just before you both go to sleep to catch up on the day or share your feelings.

2. **PLAYTIME DATES**: Set a date with your partner to play tennis together, go to the movies, lunch together or have dinner.

3. **SPECIAL DAYS, WEEKENDS OR WEEKS**: Couples need to get away without the kids. Set up a special night or, if possible, a weekend or week trip, just for yourselves. Swap childcare with a friend if you need to.

If you think you don't want to do be alone, do it anyway. But watch yourself. Couples who are not used to being alone sometimes create a fight on the way to stop the action. Once you get there and are out of your pattern of not taking time off, you'll probably have fun.

4. **CUDDLE TIME**: Watch television, listen to music or sit on the couch, touching each other with no suggestion or hint that this is the first step on the way to sex.

5. **BEDTIME**: Find time to go to bed together. This doesn't necessarily have to be at night, it could be during the day.

6. **PARALLEL PLAY**: Plan to do different activities in the house at the same time. You don't have to be doing the same thing to feel connected. Notice the difference when you are both doing separate activities and are connected versus when you are doing an activity in which you feel alone.

7. **HELPING EACH OTHER**: Find ways to help each other. This doesn't mean to just do for someone, but to ask, "Would you like me to help you?" "I'm going to the store. Is there anything you'd like me to pick up?"

SUGGESTIONS FOR GROUP SHARING

Discuss any of the activities. Share your experiences, questions or feelings.

NOTES:

AND MORE NOTES:

CHAPTER VII

LEADING A GROUP

Using this book in a group is a terrific opportunity. You don't need to be a professionally trained leader. If you can get a group of couples together to go through the activities, you'll have the opportunity to see how other couples are with each other, find out that your couple issues are ones that other couples have, and get feedback.

We recommend that you go through the book, chapter by chapter, doing the activities with the group. It's best to meet once a week for six weeks instead of a weekend. The reason is that these activities stir up a lot of thoughts and feelings. It's much better for people to get information about themselves or their spouses with a whole week to think about and deal with the feelings that come up or to try new things out without being overloaded.

We recommend the following ground rules:

1. Be honest.
2. If someone steps on your toes, say so.
3. Let your partner take care of himself/herself.
4. It's OK to pass or say "stop."
5. Share the time.

You'll want to follow the format given below because the best groups are those that stay structured. The ones that don't become a free-for-all. If, after you go through the activities, you want to meet together more informally, you'll all have some skills to help each other.

Here's the format which we suggest with time allocated for each activity. We recommend that you have a time keeper and that you stick to your schedule. It's helpful to write out your schedule and have it posted during your class. For example, 7:00 to 7:10 Introductory Activity, etc. Snacks, smoking or breaks must be added if you want to include them. This group will take every bit of the two hours scheduled.

FORMAT (For 2 Hour Group)

I. **10 Minutes   WARM-UP ACTIVITY**

We recommend a brief activity to start the group,
such as having everyone complete one of the following:

    A. The introduction to this chapter made me think
about _____ .

    or

    B. Since our last class, I learned _____.

II. **20 Minutes   INTRODUCTORY ACTIVITY**

From the chapter or make up your own.

III. **30 Minutes   LEARNING ACTIVITIES**

Depending on time, choose one or more of the
Learning Activities from the selections for that
chapter.

IV. **20 Minutes   GROUP SHARING/DISCUSSION**

Discuss the activities done in class.

V. **30 Minutes   PROBLEM SOLVING**
               (Led by the group leader.)

(Steps follow)

VI. **10 Minutes   CLOSING**

Ask members to share one of the following:

    A. I'm taking _____ with me.
    B. What stood out for me was _____.
    C. I appreciate _____.

PROBLEM SOLVING STEPS

Problem solving provides the opportunity for a group member to get help from other members. The problem does not have to be about the couple. If the issue is a couple issue, then it's the other partner's job to listen and learn about his/her partner's point of view and to let him/her do the talking.

Before you begin, ask for a volunteer to write down the problem and the suggestions made to solve it.

It's important that the leader structure this activity with the following format:

1. One person shares a problem he/she is having. If it's a couple issue, then the other partner listens and learns.

2. The person thinks of a recent example of when the problem occurred and describes it specifically so that everyone else in the group can picture who was involved, what happened and the sequence of actions that occurred.

3. The problem is role played by members of the group. The person with the presenting problem may want to role play one of the other parties in the problem. After the role play, each role player is asked how he/she felt and thought as he/she played that role. This helps to see the issue from everyone's point of view.

4. The group brainstorms alternative suggestions for dealing with this problem. The person with the problem listens. All the suggestions are written down in list form.

5. The list of alternative suggestions is read aloud, and the person with the problem chooses one of the suggestions to try during the next week. The solution is role played to see if it is effective. Role players again give feedback about feelings and thoughts. Did it work?

6. The group members give positive, specific feedback to the person who shared the problem. These are called appreciations.

NOTES:

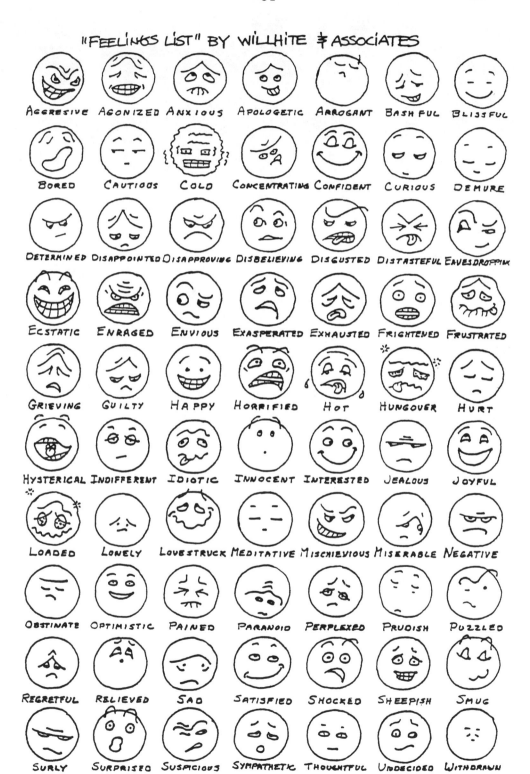

ABOUT THE AUTHORS

Lynn Lott is the founder and former Executive Director of Family Education Centers in Sonoma County, California. In addition to her private practice as a licensed Marriage, Family and Child Counselor, she is a professional speaker and conducts workshops for couples, parents, teachers, counselors and businesses. She is an Associate Professor at Sonoma State University extension.

Lynn is married and liking it. She is also the co-author of *I'm on Your Side, To Know Me Is To Love Me, Changing Your Relationship With Your Teen , Teaching Parenting, Family Work: Whose Job Is It?*, a book about family chores, and *Empowering Teenagers and Yourself in the Process Study Guide* .

Dru West is a parent educator and counselor at Family Education Centers in Petaluma, California. A Registered Intern Marriage, Family and Child Counselor, she works with individuals, couples and families.

Dru is also married and liking it. Other books Dru has co-authored include *Changing Your Relationship With Your Teen* and *To Know Me Is To Love Me*.

64

Additional copies of this book and others can be ordered from:

The Practical Press
P.O. Box 2615
Petaluma, California 94952

TITLE	PRICE	QNTY	AMOUNT
I'm On Your Side	$17.95	_____	$_____
Family Work: Whose Job Is It?	$ 9.95	_____	$_____
Together & Liking It	$ 7.95	_____	$_____
To Know Me Is To Love Me	$10.00	_____	$_____
Changing Your Relationship with Your Teen	$ 4.00	_____	$_____
Teaching Parenting	$29.95	_____	$_____
		Subtotal	$_____
		Cal. Residents add 6. % Tax	$_____
		Postage and Handling	$_____
		Total	$_____

Postage and Handling: $1.40 for first book and $.50 for each item thereafter.

MAKE CHECKS PAYABLE TO **THE PRACTICAL PRESS**

Ship To:
NAME _____

ADDRESS _____

CITY, STATE & ZIP _____

DAYTIME PHONE _____

Prices effective December, 1990 and subject to change without notice.